the romance of

CALIFORNIA VINEYARDS

the romance of

CALIFORNIA VINEYARDS

BY CARISSA CHAPPELLET   INTRODUCTION BY MOLLY CHAPPELLET

PHOTOGRAPHY BY DANIEL D'AGOSTINI

■

UNIVERSE PUBLISHING

TO THOSE WHOSE HANDS TEND THE VINES

■

Front cover: Eschen Vineyard, Amador County, Sierra Foothills
Back cover: Cabernet Sauvignon grapes
Endpapers: Grape cluster woodcut by Neil Shigley
Northern California map (detail), courtesy of *Wine Spectator*/Map design by Richard L. Thompson
First published in the United States of America in 1997 by
UNIVERSE PUBLISHING
A Division of Rizzoli International Publications, Inc.
300 Park Avenue South, New York, NY 10010
Copyright © 1997 Universe Publishing
Original text © 1997 Carissa Chappellet; Introduction © 1997 Molly Chappellet; Photography © 1997 Daniel D'Agostini

98 99 00 01/10 9 8 7 6 5 4 3 2
Library of Congress Catalog Card Number: 97-61187
Printed in Singapore

The phone numbers, addresses, and other information provided in the Vineyards to Visit, Recommended Inns,
and Recommended Restaurants sections can only be as current as the date of publication.

BOOK DESIGN BY YOLANDA CUOMO AND FRANCESCA RICHER

TABLE OF CONTENTS

■

THE ROMANCE OF CALIFORNIA VINEYARDS

∎

It simply takes one leisurely drive through the Northern California wine country to understand why it is the greatest tourist attraction in the United States after Disneyland and Disney World. What makes this region so appealing? No one can deny that it is a place of great natural beauty. But then, so are Lake Tahoe, the coast of Maine, and Yellowstone Park. So what is the particular magnetism of the vineyards of the Napa, Sonoma, and Mendocino Valleys or the Sierra Foothills? What is their siren call to visitors? As co-owner of the Chappellet Vineyard in Napa Valley, the wine country has been my home for more than thirty years; its appeal is multi-layered. We are drawn to the vines themselves, both as agriculture and near-mystical symbols of that most romantic of end-products, the wine itself. We are drawn to the history of this place, with its wonderful interweaving of European and American cultures, its family struggles, and its traditions and legacies. So, too, are we enchanted by the country's geography. The California vineyards are a veritable dictionary definition of *romantic*: "Tendency to the wonderful, mysterious, fanciful, extravagant, and wildly picturesque."

Wildly picturesque they are. Both the Napa and the northern Sonoma Valleys are narrowly carved fertile riverbeds, running north to south, protected on two sides by tree-covered mountain ranges. In the Napa Valley, the Mayacamas stand sentry to the west, the Vaca Range to the east. This simple fact of geography may explain why all of us—residents

and visitors alike—feel instantly at home here. There's a sense of peace that comes from being inside the Valley, a sense of protection and belonging. These feelings, warmed by the anticipation of that wonderful glass of wine waiting at the end of the day, are more than enough to make this one of the friendliest places on earth.

Now, my friend Daniel D'Agostini is going to take you on a personal photographic journey through the Napa, Mendocino, and Sonoma Valleys, and the Sierra Foothills, where Daniel's family owned California's third-oldest winery—a journey enlivened by his passion for vineyards and his ability to translate that passion into images that capture the appeal of this place we both call "home." Since most people have only visited the wine country during a single season, Daniel has chosen to show us the vineyards in all seasons— in all light. My daughter Carissa's texts, along with collected quotes from vintners, viticulturists, and writers, complement Daniel's images. Hers is an insider's perspective, one cultivated by years living and growing up on a vineyard.

While the California wine country is full of life, it is also redolent of the past. A couple of hundred years ago this land belonged to Native Americans and to the redwoods. The runoff from Mount Saint Helena, at 4,500 feet, fed sparkling brooks. Bucks, bear, coyote, mountain lions, and rattlesnakes abounded. By 1850, with the Gold Rush transforming the West, there were blacksmiths, chemists, Chinese launderers, stage drivers, and highwaymen. Soon the geysers and sulphur springs which served as healing grounds for the Indians began to attract wealthy San Franciscans in search of weekend spa retreats. This was the age of the railroad, and its tracks running parallel to the main highway were the great arteries of transportation and communication.

But venerable as the recent history of the Valley may seem, it is a moment in time compared to the grander history of grapes. Most historians believe that the cultivation— and enjoyment—of grapes dates back about 7,000 years. Egyptian frescoes depict grapes and wine drinking. The ancient Greeks used amphoras to store wine, and the enjoyment of wine drinking is captured in art adorning many of their vessels. It was around 1500 B.C. that wine finally arrived in Italy, and soon after in France and Spain.

When the Spanish began traveling to the New World, they brought vines to plant in their mission vineyards. In the 1830s, the first vines were planted at the Franciscan Mission in what was to become Sonoma. It was this mission that served as headquarters to Mariano Guadalupe Vallejo during his term as governor of Mexico. Even after the Bear Flag Revolt of 1846 and the end of the Mexican regime, General Vallejo stayed on in this seductive valley where he eventually acquired 80,000 acres of land and began to cultivate grapes. He was matched in his enterprise by his neighbor and friendly competitor, the Hungarian Agoston Haraszthy, who imported more than 100,000 vines from Europe and established the Buena Vista Winery in 1857. It was Haraszthy who became known as the "father of modern viticulture." He was soon joined in the ranks of innovators by the German Charles Krug, who had worked with Haraszthy. Krug became legendary when he borrowed Haraszthy's cider press and subsequently became the first winemaker to crush grapes in the Napa Valley with something other than feet. Other founders of the industry included Captain Gustave Niebaum of Inglenook, Jacob Schram, who established a winery later known as Schramsberg, James Korbel, Jacob and Frederick Beringer, and Georges de Latour of Beaulieu.

In the 1860s wine was big business. Ten and one-half million vines were producing grapes. By 1869 the Union Pacific Railroad facilitated the exportation of wine to the east coast and to Europe. In fact, the California wine, Schramsberger Hock, was served in the best London clubs, while other California wines were taking prizes in Europe. As is the case in all lucrative endeavors, prosperous businessmen were entering the scene. For instance, James Fair, a wealthy senator, had vineyards in Petaluma; George Hearst of *The San Francisco*

Examiner cultivated grapes in Sonoma; railroad magnate Leland Stanford had large vineyards in San Jose and Sacramento.

Prohibition was devastating to most wineries, causing many to close their doors. But some wineries were able to operate by making sacramental wines or by selling grapes to home winemakers. Most of the low-yielding, better wine grapes were uprooted or regrafted to heavy-yielding juice grapes, such as Alicante Bouschet—its tougher skins made it suitable for shipping.

When Prohibition ended in 1933, the scene drastically changed. Only a very few wineries, such as Beaulieu, had been able to cellar their wines. In fact, the reputation of Beaulieu was made by having their vintage ten-year-old Cabernets to release to the market. Despite Beaulieu's good fortune, the wine industry in general struggled tremendously. The new plantings of good varietals took a few years to come into fruition and then into production. It wasn't until the 1940s and 1950s that fine wines were being distributed by a handful of the old guard—Beaulieu, Martini, Krug, Inglenook, to name a few. Still remembered today are Beaulieu's Private Reserve Cabernet 1947 and 1951 (made by André Tchelistcheff), as well as the great Cabernets from Inglenook.

Shortly thereafter, other new wineries of a smaller scale began producing outstanding wines. While Stony Hill created a new style Chardonnay, Hanzell in Sonoma, using imported French oak barrels, brought Burgundian flavors to Chardonnay and Pinot Noir. Inspired by these great California wines, a few young families moved to the Napa Valley to make their mark. Joe Heitz brought his expertise and his technical skills; Robert Mondavi set out on his own and began building the Robert Mondavi Winery; Jack Davies and Bob Travers revived the old wineries of Schramsberg and Mayacamas; and Donn Chappellet, with his business skills and love of great wines, established the Chappellet Winery with a hillside vineyard. But, despite the growth, at this time there were still only about thirty wineries in the area. Today the Napa Valley has close to 300, and California has over 800.

But it was a Paris wine tasting in 1976 that attracted world-wide attention to the California wines. In a blind tasting with only French judges, a California wine, Chateau Montelena's 1973 Chardonnay, was awarded first place, as was the Cabernet Sauvignon of the Stag's Leap Wine Cellars.

The 1970s and 1980s were exciting years for wine lovers. More small wineries, including Caymus, Diamond Creek, and the Grace Family Vineyard, joined the quest for excellent wines. Other wineries, such as Opus One, a joint effort of Mondavi and Rothchild, formed international partnerships.

Of course, history has its own cycles, and that is certainly exemplified in the wine industry of Northern California. In the 1870s, the phylloxera root louse attacked the vines, subjecting them to the same damage many of ours are facing today. Around that same time, an international economic depression wiped out many vineyards. Similarly, recent economic events have forced many vineyards to be sold or to file for Chapter 11 protection—just as the industry had finally recovered from half a century of the reeling effects of Prohibition. And today, as in the 1860s, big business has once again recognized the potential of California winemaking—Nestlé, Heublein, Coca-Cola, Seagrams, and other conglomerates have entered the scene by purchasing existing wineries.

When we first moved to the Napa Valley in 1967, prune, almond, and walnut orchards held their place alongside the vineyards. Cattle, horses, goats, and sheep were our neighbors, and the olive leaves shimmered silver on the hillsides and along the driveways of some of the older homes and ranches. There were only about 12,000 acres of grapes. As farmers, we all worried about the damage developers could do to the agricultural nature of the Valley. Had it not been for the Agricultural Preserve, which keeps farmland from being sold in small parcels, present-day visitors might well be looking at a sea of houses instead of vineyards. Over the years, the restrictions on subdividing have become even more stringent.

Today virtually every square inch of land seems to be covered with grapevines bordered by olive trees, and new vineyards are appearing in the hills all the time. But what is most exciting to those of us who make our living in the vineyards is the quality of wines being produced. Available now, more than ever before, is a constantly increasing variety of wines made with great finesse and character. In fact, it is difficult to find a bad bottle of wine in the area. After considerable experimentation in winemaking in the late 1970s and 1980s, emphasis has once again returned to its proper place: the grape. Today, the quest of each vineyard is to find the "right" grape, or the best variety for a particular climate, exposure, and soil condition. We obsess about soil in the valleys. It determines which root stock to plant, which varietal to cultivate, and which clone will do best. We pay attention to the number of sun hours, elevation, and frost risks. We weigh all those factors in deciding what, when, and how to plant, and how best to train and prune the vines.

Vineyardists are continuously designing radical systems of trellising in order to make the best possible use of the plant, and to yield the best quality fruit. In some cases wind machines that used to protect vines from frost are being replaced by automatic irrigation systems that go on when the temperature drops below a certain point. The water coats the vines and freezes, insulating the plant from more cold. In addition to all this, there are numerous methods of groundscape, from discing to planting cover crops, which help prevent erosion and add nutrients back to the soil.

In the end, however, grape growers are still farmers, and like all farmers we are at the mercy of Mother Nature. We hold our collective breath in early spring, just after the new shoots have appeared, knowing that a frost then can be deadly. Winds that come before the canes have been tied can break major branches or cause damage at the time of flowering. Mostly we love rain, but at blossom or harvest time it can be disastrous. And, to add to the dangers sent from the heavens, lurking diseases are ready at any moment to threaten our beloved vineyards.

On top of the farmers' problems, the vintner has the additional apprehension of not knowing whether he has truly selected the right grape for a particular location for seven to ten years—or longer. It takes grapevines a minimum of four years to produce a crop and some wines require at least three years to be ready to market, depending on the variety. But the seventh year only gives us a glimpse of what that varietal might offer. It is, after all, only *one* vintage, made from very young vines. It will take a number of vintages before we know if we have made a good choice.

A vineyard is an undeniably romantic place, as Daniel's photographs so poignantly illustrate. But it is also a place of constant work and more than a little worry. Knowing how a vineyard works and how fragile each vintage can be, makes all of us even more respectful of the wine country's beauty and romance. It makes us appreciate the sheer, sensual quality of the vines themselves—in every season. They are spare and sculptural when dormant, evocative and full of promise when the tender green leaves begin to appear, then lush and full as the season unfolds, until they are heavy, ripe, and fragrant with fruit, and finally red and gold as autumn begins to chill the air. There is no season in these valleys that does not move my soul.

And at the end of it all is the wine itself, a reward and an incentive for our painstaking work. It does not matter what size acreage or what size winery—it can be only an acre or hundreds of acres—it's the passion, knowledge, and dedication of the vintner that produces a work of art. Each wine carries to our palate its own history, the nuances of the land, and the character of the grape. We value our land in a way Robert Louis Stevenson explained so well:

> Those lodes and pockets of earth more precious than the precious ores, that yield
> inimitable fragrance and soft fire, whose virtuous bonanzas, where the soil has
> sublimated under sun and stars to something finer and the wine is bottled poetry.

Vineyards have to be the most beautiful
form of agriculture. They have the linear quality
I love in other forms of row crops. And
they have a unique advantage: you don't have
to replant them each season. . .

■

MOLLY CHAPPELLET

The historic fieldstone cellar, built in 1872 at Boeger Winery, sits
at 2,100 feet up in the Sierra Foothills. Boeger's current production, from thirty-five acres of
vineyards, includes Cabernet, Zinfandel, Barbera, and Merlot.

Making wine is a skill—fine wine an art. That's been

my motto from the beginning. Like art, wine is a form

of communication; it responds to commitment

and discipline on the part of the winemaker; and the consumer's

pleasure takes many forms. At Robert Mondavi Winery,

we present our wines in company with

various other arts—music, painting, sculpture,

and drama—because we believe that all fine wine belongs in

the company of great art.

■

ROBERT MONDAVI

The Robert Mondavi Winery lies in the heart of the Napa Valley. Many say that
Robert Mondavi is, indeed, the heart of the Valley. The mission-style architecture of the winery, designed
by Cliff May in the mid-1960s, includes a majestic tower which beckons travelers into the
region. Mondavi's success is renowned—his reserve wines compete with the finest wines in the world.

Trellises of grapes accent the rolling hills of the Shenandoah Valley in the Sierra Foothills where the Karly Winery is located—an area known for producing Zinfandel. Throughout the wine country are the families who create the wineries. Karly Winery was started and is still run by Karly Cobb and her husband Larry "Buck" Cobb. Karly loves to cook and has an oven in their tasting room where she bakes sourdough bread on the weekends. ∎

Different approaches to planting and trellising are noticeable throughout the vineyards. In new plantings, we see a greater density of vines and a closer spacing of rows. A vertical trellis that weaves canes up between wires, so that the fruit is more exposed to the sun, can be observed. And the Geneva double curtain, a T-support on the taller stakes with two extended arms, creating a V-shape that leaves the center exposed to more light and air, is sometimes visible.

In some of today's small wine operations, wooden lugs are still used for grapepicking.
The winter months provide a time for mending the lugs.

The first formations of grapes appear as tiny upright clusters of berries.
At this stage viticulturists may eliminate some of the berry clusters so that the energy of the
plant is directed to maturing fewer grapes and allowing a more "even" ripening.

i would not have every man, or every part
of a man, cultivated, any more than
I would have every acre of earth cultivated:
part will be tillage, but the greater part
will be meadow and forest, not only
serving an immediate use, but preparing a
mould against a distant future, by the
annual decay of the vegetation it supports.

◼

HENRY DAVID THOREAU

In 1989 the Barrelli Creek Vineyard, located in the Alexander
Valley of Sonoma County, was purchased by Ernest and
Julio Gallo. This land was first planted with grapes in 1861,
but later was left to pasture. The Gallo Winery is now
completing a replanting of 625 acres here with myriad varietals.
The distinctive plantings include Merlot, Cabernet Sauvignon,
Cabernet Franc, Zinfandel, Petite Syrah, Sangiovese, Barbera,
Sauvignon Blanc, and Chardonnay. The Gallo Winery is
committed to the land and its use. As Julio Gallo would often say,
"For every acre of grapes we plant, we preserve an acre of land
for wildlife, habitat, watersheds, and beauty." This ideal
has become company policy. For every new vineyard planted, 50
percent of the land is held aside as a natural habitat.

For all the style and glamour of its market image, its
roots are in the earth . . . . Wine is one of the
miracles of nature, and . . . its 10,000 years
of partnership with man has not removed that
element of mystery, that independent life that alone
among all our foods has made men
think of it as divine.

HUGH JOHNSON

The dramatic trellised entrance to the Rutherford Hill
caves sets the mood for an enthralling visit into the mountainside where their
wines are cellared. Located in the Napa Valley, this winery is
known for its Merlot and Cabernet.

H ere, the Light is
mingled with shadow.
Do you want your light
totally pure?

∎

RUMI

A misty fog rolls in at dusk at
Handley Cellars' vineyards, in the Anderson
and Dry Creek Valleys. Founded in 1982,
this vineyard of twenty-eight acres
sits in the extreme northwest wine growing
areas of Mendocino County. This
region is ideal for Pinot Noir,
Gewürztraminer, and Riesling. At
Handley, modern sustainable vineyard
management utilizes cover crops such as
lupine, fava beans, clovers, vetch,
and other nitrogen-fixing legumes to build
soil fertility, while minimizing
erosion and reducing dust.

I look at things for their shape,

for their color,

for their form,

and with that point of view

they become new and different—

exciting even.

GERD VERSCHOOR

Imaginative uses for bottles, corks, grape stakes,
and labels are found everywhere in the wine country. At Napa
Valley's di Rosa Preserve a structure made of
hundreds of discarded wine bottles adorns the property.

Previous spread: Grapes must be crushed
immediately after picking
in order to avoid oxidation and deterioration. Potter
Vineyard's grapes are being tossed into a crusher
at Amador Foothill Winery in the Shenandoah Valley of
the Sierra Foothills.

R ocks are a huge issue when developing a vineyard.
In preparing the land for planting,
the soil is "ripped" down thirty inches with a tractor.
We remove all the rocks, from the size of an
orange to the size of a van. However, the rock is still the best part of
our land, adding important minerals to the soil, while it
allows the rain to drain through quickly
in the spring, encouraging an early bud break.

■

DAVE PIRIO
Chappellet's Viticulturist

Rambling rock walls, as seen here at the edge of Chappellet's vineyard, are a common site throughout
the Napa Valley. The decorative walls provide a place to put rocks that
are cleared from the vineyards during planting. They also serve as retaining walls to
prevent erosion or as guard rails over bridges.

In the winter, before pruning, the vines seem to be living a life of their own, gesturing to one another with their wispy arms.

■

CARISSA CHAPPELLET

The manner of pruning the vines affects the yield and quality of the next crop. The fruit for the following year develops from the current buds on the canes. "Head-pruning," a traditional method of training grapes used at many of the older vineyards, is rapidly falling out of fashion. Instead, trellising techniques have greatly advanced the growth and "even" ripening of the grapes.

When you stand in our mountain vineyards, the vines in
every direction are thrilling and absorbing!
Mountains, forests, vineyards. And at night! The dramatic
moon and stars shedding light all around us.
It's not just romantic, it's magical!

■

JAMIE DAVIES

Schramsberg Vineyards, Calistoga, Napa Valley, known for their outstanding
champagnes, also boasts a picturesque olive grove. Jack and Jamie Davies began the winery in 1965,
naming it after Jacob Schram, who made his wines here in 1862.

If you really want to make great
wine, go to the hills. Farming will cost you
more, but it will be worth it.

ANDRE TCHELISTCHEFF

After the grapes have been pressed, what remains are seeds and skin.
This remnant, known as pomace, is a fabulous mulch which is reused in the vineyards,
or, when it can be spared, in private gardens.

What potent blood hath modest May!

RALPH WALDO EMERSON

Fermented crushed grapes flow through a hose into the
press at Amador Foothill Winery. The rich color of the juice comes
from the pigmentation of grape skin.
This Shenandoah Valley winery specializes in Zinfandel.

Previous spread: Many vineyards in the Napa and Sonoma Valleys,
such as the Cuvaison Vineyards of Carneros, have ponds or
reservoirs to hold water for irrigating new vines. Cuvaison is well-known
for their Reserve Carneros Chardonnay.

Having known and enjoyed the Napa Valley for
thirty-two years, and having seen the old
plum and walnut orchards give way to increasingly fine
vineyards, today we revel in its lush beauty,
its glorious wines, and the magic of old friendships.

■

ARTHUR AND SHEILA HAILEY

Since vast acreages of rural farmland have been transformed into vineyards in the last twenty-five years,
very few old barns remain in the Northern California winemaking region.

Let us
get up early to
the vineyards;
let us see
if the vine
flourish,
whether the
tender grape
appear?

■

SONG OF
SOLOMON 7:12

Beringer Knight's
Valley Vineyard,
Sonoma County

ld fashioned, hand-cranked presses are still used in many wineries, such as at Black Sheep in the Sierra Foothills, when batches of grapes are too small to go through an electric press. The Black Sheep Winery's production includes Cabernet, Zinfandel, Sauvignon Blanc, and Chenin Blanc.

Sometimes I feel as if we need a musical
composition about the progress of the vines, piped
through the streets, letting the visitors
know what's really going on in the vineyard.

■

MOLLY CHAPPELLET

Birds find that a grapevine makes a great place to build a nest here at Sonoma Valley's
Buena Vista Winery. Founded in 1857 by Agostan Haraszthy, it is one of the oldest vineyards in the United States.
A new winery was built in the late 1970s by the A. Raacke Company, which produces more than 200,000
cases, utilizing grapes from nearly 935 acres.

M

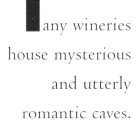

any wineries
house mysterious
and utterly
romantic caves.

JAN SHREM
Clos Pegase, Napa Valley

Wine caves, like those at Napa Valley's Araujo Estate Winery,
provide an ideal environment for aging wine. The aging
process necessitates the cool, constant temperature of 52°F,
which is naturally maintained in the caves. This stellar,
new winery is the home for the grapes from the Eisele
Vineyard, a premier Cabernet vineyard, purchased by
Daphne and Bart Araujo in 1990.

With over 135 years of experience,
we are in favor of those relationships that one
expects to endure forever. . . .

■

MARK MONDAVI

Founded in 1861, the Charles Krug Winery was the first winery in the
Napa Valley. In 1943, it was purchased by the Mondavi family. With nearly 1,000 acres, its production
now includes Merlot, Chardonnay, and Pinot Noir, among other varietals.

I n the center of Napa Valley is the picturesque Sutter Home Winery, located in St. Helena, which was founded in 1874. More than 800 varieties of flowers and herbs surround the old family home, which is now used as a bed and breakfast. Producing five million cases of wine from roughly 2,500 acres of vineyards, the winery's success came largely in 1972 from their production of white Zinfandel. This "blush" wine, with its hint of sweetness, captured wide appeal among new wine drinkers.

A technique used at the Beringer Knight's Valley Vineyard for new plantings—plastic
translucent cylinders encircling young vines—fosters the rapid
growth of the vines, while it also protects them from rabbits and deer. Often
milk or juice cartons are used instead of plastic tubing.

While the practice of farming with draft horses at Bellerose Vineyards
in Sonoma County may seem charming, it was a lot of hard work. Today, narrow tractors
are used on this small, terraced hillside vineyard.

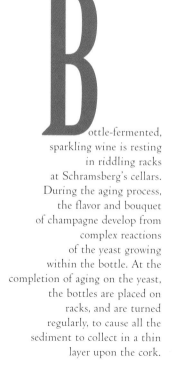

Bottle-fermented,
sparkling wine is resting
in riddling racks
at Schramsberg's cellars.
During the aging process,
the flavor and bouquet
of champagne develop from
complex reactions
of the yeast growing
within the bottle. At the
completion of aging on the yeast,
the bottles are placed on
racks, and are turned
regularly, to cause all the
sediment to collect in a thin
layer upon the cork.

*V*ines are like people—each so individualistic.
I find myself talking to them. I love
to walk in the vineyards, smell the earth,
and watch the drama of nature.

■

ELEANOR COPPOLA
Niebaum-Coppola Vineyard and Winery, Napa Valley

A 130-year-old, gnarled grapevine is silhouetted against a
magnificent sky at the Grand-Père Vineyard, Shenandoah Valley in the Sierra Foothills.
Years of "head pruning" have resulted in thick, strong arms on the
vine which support the heavy fruit without the aid of stakes and guidewires.

there is a quiet
peacefulness when
winter comes
to the Napa Valley.
The dormant
vines enjoy the cold,
but when spring
comes and tender new
shoots appear,
freezing temperatures
can be disastrous.

MOLLY CHAPPELLET

We have been farming Sobon Estate organically for five years, and the vineyard is non-irrigated. We have separated out two of the oldest blocks of vines, each growing on distinctly different soils, and are using the grapes to make award-winning Zinfandels. One vineyard, situated on a prehistoric volcanic flow, is called "Rocky Top"; the other is named "Cougar Hill," after the mountain lion who is occasionally spotted there.

■

LEON SOBON

The old entrance to Sobon Estate is found at the base of the Sierra Nevada Mountains, an old California grape-growing region known as the Sierra Foothills. Formerly called D'Agostini Winery, Sobon was originally founded in 1856, making it one of the oldest wineries in California.

The grapes, after picking, are de-stemmed
and pumped into a fermenting tank,
where it will take several weeks for the
color in the skins to bleed out
into the juice. The grapes will then
be pressed to remove the skins
and seeds, and the juice will be pumped
into the tanks or small oak barrels,
where it will remain for up
to two years prior to bottling.

In some small wineries,
steel tubs are used in the aeration
stage of fermentation.

Whenever he feels the god's paradigm grip his throat,
the voice does not die in his mouth. All becomes vineyard, all becomes
grape, ripened on the hills of his sensuous South.

For he is a herald who is with us always, holding far into the doors
of the dead a bowl with ripe fruit worthy of praise.

RAINER MARIA RILKE

A harvester at Stevenot Winery, Sierra Foothills, shows off the red grapes cut with the curved blade of his
picking knife. This small winery of twenty acres was established in 1978.

A striking stone-framed window at Napa Valley's Peju Province Winery illustrates the extent to
which owner Tony Peju went to keep the buildings in harmony with nature. Peju underwent a long struggle
in getting permission to build this recent winery—the county's building guidelines have
become exceedingly rigid due to the incredible growth of the Valley in the past fifteen years.

W

hat's new in our vineyards? Everything! Due to phylloxera we've had to replant all of our vineyards! That means new rootstock, trellis systems, spacing, and in some cases a complete rethinking of what variety will grow best for the location.

■

DENNIS CAKEBREAD
Cakebread Cellars, Napa Valley

Phylloxera, a louse that attacks the roots of vines, is a reoccurring disaster for winegrowers world-wide. The infested plants need to be pulled out and replanted. Traveling through the soil it spreads quickly from vineyard to vineyard. In the 1860s, phylloxera virtually wiped out the French winemaking industry. California vineyards were first hit in the late 1800s and then again in the Napa Valley in the 1980s. Nearly 70 percent of the vineyards were forced to replant.

Amador County in spring
is an incredibly romantic place. The
gentle rolling hills are as vibrant a green
as you can imagine; the open fields
and roadsides are lined with
beautiful blue lupines, California
poppies, and a plethora of
magenta, lavender, pink,
and yellow wild flowers. Walking
through Amador County
in the springtime
is like strolling through
an enormous landscaped park.

■

JEFFREY MEYERS
Montevina Vineyards, Amador County

VINEYARDS TO VISIT

As this book has shown you glimpses into the life behind the wines—the vineyards themselves—you may now be curious to step onto these soils yourself. Here is a list of some of the vineyards that you can visit; many have picnic areas. Noted is a special wine from each winery to enjoy on your picnic.

V = Vineyard visit. P = Picnic area.

MENDOCINO

(V/P) Fetzer (Zinfandel Mendocino County Reserve)
(P) Greenwood Ridge Vineyards (Pinot Noir Anderson Valley)
(V by appt./P) Handley Cellars (Pinot Meunier)
(V/P) Husch Vineyards (Sauvignon Blanc Mendocino County La Ribera Ranch)
(P) McDowell Valley Vineyards (Valley Estate Reserve Syrah)
(P) Navarro Vineyards (Dry Style Gewürztraminer Estate Bottled)
(P) Obester Winery (Gewürztraminer Anderson Valley)
(P) Parducci Wine Cellar (Petite Syrah)
(V by appt./P) Scharffenberger Cellars (Sparkling Wine Mendocino County Blanc de Blancs)

NAPA

(V) Cakebread Cellars (Cabernet Sauvignon)
(P by appt.) Chappellet (Old Vine Cuvée, Barrel Fermented)
(P) Clos Du Val Wine Company (Cabernet Sauvignon)
(P) Clos Pegase Winery (Chardonnay)
(P) Cuvaison (Chardonnay Carneros Reserve)
(P) Flora Springs Winery (Chardonnay, Barrel Fermented/Trilogy)
(V) Freemark Abbey (Johannisberg Riesling Edelwein Gold)
(V/P) Charles Krug Winery (Chardonnay Carneros Reserve)
(P) Louis Martini Winery (Muscato)
(V) Robert Mondavi Winery (Pinot Noir Private Reserve)
(V by appt.) Joseph Phelps Vineyard (The Insignia)
(P) Rutherford Hill (Merlot)
(V/P) St. Suprey Vineyards (Sauvignon Blanc)
(V) Trefethen Vineyards (Trefethen Estate Chardonnay)

SIERRA FOOTHILLS

(P) Amador Foothill Winery (Sangiovese)
(P) Boeger Winery (Barbera)
(V by appt./P) Chateau Rodin Winery (Zinfandel El Dorado)
(P) Chatom Vineyards (Sauvignon Blanc Reserve Calaveras County)
(P) Deaver Vineyards (Zinfandel)
(V by appt./P) Karly Winery (Syrah or Marsanne)
(P) Montevina Winery (Terra d'Oro Zinfandel)
(V by appt./P) Sierra Vista (Rhone Varietals)
(P) Sobon Estate (Syrah Shenandoah Valley)
(P) Stevenot Winery (Cabernet Sauvignon Reserve)

SONOMA

(V/P) Benzinger Family Winery (Estate grown Reserve Cabernet)
(P by appt.) Buena Vista Vineyards (Lake County Sauvignon Blanc)
(P) Chateau St. Jean Vineyards (Chardonnay Alexander Valley Robert Young Vineyard Reserve)
(V by appt./P) Cline Cellars (Jaccuzzi Zinfandel)
(P) Dry Creek Vineyard (Meritage Red Dry Creek Valley)
(V by appt./P) Field Stone Winery and Vineyard (Petite Sirah)
(V/P) Foppiano Vineyards (Petite Sirah)
(P) J. Fritz Winery (Late Harvest Zinfandel)
(P) Geyser Peak Winery (Reserve Shiraz)
(V/P) Gloria Ferrer Champagne Caves (Royal Cuvée)
(P) Gundlach-Bundschu Winery (Zinfandel Sonoma Valley)
(P) Hop Kiln Winery (Zinfandel Russian River Valley Primitivo Reserve)
(V/P) Kunde Estate Winery (Viognier Sonoma Valley)
(P) Matanzas Creek Winery (Chardonnay)
(V/P) Sebastiani Vineyards (Cherryblock Cabernet)
(V by appt./P) Simi Winery (Chardonnay Sonoma County Reserve)
(P) Trentadau Winery and Vineyards (Old Patch Red)
(P) Viansa Winery (Cabernet Blend Napa-Sonoma Counties Riserva)

RECOMMENDED INNS

With all of its well-known tourist attractions, California is still a place in which one can discover hidden treasures. As you head out to find the romantic vineyards depicted in this book, here are a few special inns we recommend. We've listed only the lesser-known small inns; although places such as Rancho Caymus, The Wine Country Inn, Meadowood, AuBerge du Soleil, The Madrona Manor, and The Heritage House should not be missed on your travels through the wine country.

MENDOCINO AND SONOMA COUNTIES

THE APPLE FARM
Hosts: Karen Bates and Sally Schmitt (formerly of The French Laundry)
18501 Greenwood Rd., Philo, CA 95466
(707) 895–2333 or (707) 895–2461
Visit The Apple Farm fruit stand. Fabulous cooking classes. One room located above cooking demonstration kitchen and dining room. Country look, with a delightful vegetable and ornamental garden.

BOONVILLE HOTEL AND RESTAURANT
Chef/Owner: John Schmitt
P.O. Box 326, Boonville, CA 95415
(707) 895–2210
Beautiful rooms with country-style, handmade wooden beds. Great dinners including unusual Mexican fare; lunches served in the summer.

MANKAS INVERNESS
Owner: Margaret Gradé
P.O. Box 1110, Inverness, CA 94973
(415) 669–1034
Nine rooms. Charming, rustic, formerly a hunting lodge. Accommodations are cozy—down comforters and feather beds. Superb cuisine; wonderful wine list.

PHILO POTTERY INN
Hosts: Barry and Sue Chiverton
8550 Hwy. 128, Philo, CA 95466

(707) 895–3069
B&B with five rooms. 1888 redwood farmhouse. Great breakfasts, cozy rooms, bike trails. Near Anderson Valley wineries and Mendocino coast.

NAPA VALLEY

CALISTOGA

SCARLETT'S COUNTRY INN
Host: Scarlett Dwyer
3918 Silverado Trail,
Calistoga, CA 94515
(707) 942–6669
Located off the Silverado Trail. Casual, wooded retreat, with a pool.

ZINFANDEL HOUSE
Hosts: George and Betty Starke
1253 Summit Dr., Calistoga, CA 94515
(707) 942–0733
Great hosts! Magnificent views of the valley. Three very comfortable, unpretentious rooms.

For those who want the bed and breakfast experience, but need to be right in town, here are two lovely inns in Calistoga:

THE ELMS
Hosts: Stephen and Karla Wyle
1300 Cedar St., Calistoga, CA 94515
(707) 942–9476
Six rooms. Beautiful, grand Victorian home surrounded by the largest elm trees in Napa Valley.

LA CHAUMIERE
Host: Gary Venturi
1301 Cedar St., Calistoga, CA 94515
(707) 942–5139
Three rooms. Intimate front garden; cottage-style home; gourmet breakfasts, and hors d'oeuvres.

NAPA

BROOKSIDE VINEYARD B&B
Hosts: Susan and Tom Ridley
3194 Redwood Rd., Napa, CA 94558
(707) 944–1661
Three rooms. It's hard to be any more

in the heart of what's wonderful about wine country than at this secret place. Situated with a vineyard on two sides, gardens, and a babbling brook at the back, it is total immersion.

CREEKSIDE INN
Owners/Hosts: Ginger and Sara Toogood
945 Main Street, St. Helena, CA 94574
(707) 963–7244
Charming country house within walking distance of St. Helena. Exceptional breakfast.

OAK KNOLL INN
Host: Barbara Possino
2200 Oak Knoll Ave.
Napa, CA 94558 (707) 255–2200
Four rooms. A personal itinerary is prepared for each guest. Elegant rooms surrounded by expansive vineyards. A luxurious well-deserved experience.

TRUBODY RANCH
Hosts: Jeff and Mary Page
5444 St. Helena Hwy.,
Napa, CA 94558
(707) 255–5907
Original ranch property; two rooms in an old water tower. Uncluttered, open spaces furnished with original Trubody family antiques. Surrounded by vineyards on all sides.

ST. HELENA

DEER RUN
Hosts: Tom and Carol Wilson
3995 Spring Mountain Rd.,
St. Helena, CA 94574
(707) 963–3794
Separate bungalows. High atop the prettiest country road you're ever likely to see.

VILLA ST. HELENA
Host: Ralph Cotton
2727 Sulfur Springs Ave., St. Helena, CA 94574 (707) 963–2514
Long winding ascent through beautiful forests. Grassy meadows; fabulous views. A unique villa.

RECOMMENDED RESTAURANTS

Great wines demand great food, and so you'll find dozens of fabulous eating spots throughout the wine regions of Northern California. Here is a list of a few of our favorites you might not have found on your own.

MENDOCINO COUNTY

CAFE BEAUJOLAIS
Chefs/Owners: Christopher Kump and Margaret Fox
961 Ukiah St., Mendocino, CA 95460
(707) 937–5614
Cozy dining room with innovative American cuisine.

HERITAGE HOUSE
Chef: Lance Dean Velasquez
5200 N. Hwy. 1, Little River
CA 95456 (707) 937–5885
Serves delightful French country food.

MOOSSE CAFE
Owner: Linda Friedman
390 Kasten St., Mendocino
CA 95460 (707) 937–4323
Lovely lunch. Eclectic menu from steaks and potatoes to Asian cuisine.

PANGAEA
Owner/Chef: Shannon Hughes
250 Main St., Point Arena, CA 95468
(707) 882–3001
Wednesday—Sunday dinner.
Local organic fruits and vegetables; homebaked breads. Widely eclectic menu.

NAPA VALLEY

ALL SEASONS CAFE
Owners: Gayle Keller and Alex Dierkhising
1400 Lincoln Ave., Calistoga, CA 94515
(707) 942–9111
Good light fare; great soups and salads. California bistro-style cuisine.

AUBERGE DU SOLEIL
Executive Chef: Andrew Sutton
180 Rutherford Hill Rd., Rutherford, CA 94573 (707) 963–1211
Wonderful, serene breakfast overlooking the Valley. Always a special treat. Mixed fare: Southwestern, Italian, Texan, and Asian influences. Try the salmon sushimi or roasted lobster sausage appetizers. The roasted rack of lamb entrée is excellent.

BISTRO DON GIOVANNI
Chefs/Owners: Giovanni and Donna Scala
Executive Chef: Catherine Cora
4110 St. Helena Hwy., Napa, CA 94559 (707) 224–3300
Creative, fabulous food with Italian emphasis. Fun!

CATAHOULA RESTAURANT & SALOON
Owner/Chef: Jan Birnbaum
1457 Lincoln Ave., Calistoga, CA 94515
(707) 942-2275
With crème fraîche in the mashed potatoes, you know you're being spoiled! Outstanding, original, Louisiana-style food with great seasoning.

DOMAINE CHANDON
Chef: Philippe Jeanty
1 California Dr., Yountville, CA 94599
(707) 944–2892
Lunch on terrace. California cuisine with French roots. Everything on the menu is excellent. Try the house smoked trout.

FOOTHILL CAFE
Chef: Jerry Shaffer
2766 Old Sonoma Rd., Napa, CA 94559 (707) 252–6178
Off the beaten track, but well worth it! Seasonal, regional cooking. Oak oven— good smoked foods.

THE FRENCH LAUNDRY
Owner/Chef: Thomas Keller
6640 Washington St., Yountville, CA 94599 (707) 944–2380
Outstanding! Elegant. Creative American cuisine with a French influence in a charming, old stone building. Thomas Keller won James Beard's Most Outstanding Chef Award in 1997. Try the chef's tasting menu with nine courses—a great variety of small tastes in one meal.

GORDON'S CAFE
Qwner/Chef: Sally Gordon
6770 Washington St., Yountville, CA 94599 (707) 944–8246
A new Napa Valley secret. Old-fashioned country store that now serves breakfast and lunch. Great scones.

GREEN VALLEY CAFE
Chefs/Owners: Delio and Chrieo Cuneo
1310 Main St., St. Helena, CA 94574
(707) 963–7088
Small, intimate feeling. Good Italian dinners at reasonable rates.

THE RESTAURANT AT MEADOWOOD
Chef: Roy Breiman
900 Meadowood Lane, St. Helena, CA 94574 (707) 963–3646
Lunch on terrace. Beautiful environment; relaxing. Consistently good food. Great hamburgers! Separate, low-fat spa menu.

MUSTARD'S GRILL
Owner/Chef: Cindy Pawlcyn
7399 St. Helena Hwy., Yountville, CA 94558 (707) 944–2424
Very talented chef. Always something new and excellent! An "American roadside café" featuring double-cut pork chops with hoisin marinade, stuffed roasted Mexican peppers, chicken satay, and duck.

OAKVILLE GROCERY
Owner: Joseph Phelps
7856 St. Helena Hwy., Oakville, CA 94562 (707) 944-8802
Wonderful gourmet shop in old-fashioned grocery store.

PINOT BLANC

Executive Chef: Joachim Splichal
Chef: Shawn Knight
641 Main St., St. Helena, CA 94574
(707) 963–6191
Marvelous French country bistro.
Joachim elevates potatoes to a new
level. Simple ingredients with
complex flavors. Most romantic
outside eating in the Valley.

TERRA

Chefs/Owners: Hiro Stone
and Lissa Doumani
1345 Railroad Ave., St. Helena, CA
94574 (707) 963–8931
Always superb! East-West cuisine.
Inviting atmosphere; old stone building.

TRA VIGNE

Chef/Partner: Michael Chiarello
Managing Partner: Kevin Cronin
1050 Charter Oak St., St. Helena, CA
94574 (707) 963–4440
Delicious Californian-Italian fare.
Lunch in the courtyard or dinner on
the terrace is perfection. Try the
eggplant bruschetta. For dessert, have
the Budino di Cioccolata (warm
chocolate brownie custard).

TRILOGY

Owner/Chef: Diane and Don Pariseau
1234 Main St., St. Helena, CA 94574
(707) 963–5507
Outstanding Californian-French style
food. Very small and intimate. Menu
changes daily. Three-course prix fixe
menu is available with matching wines.

WAPPO BAR & BISTRO

Chefs/Owners: Michelle Mutrux
and Aaron Bauman.
1226–B Washington St., Calistoga, CA
94515 (707) 942–4712
Charming patio. Diverse menu with a
Mediterranean flair, and a bit of spice.
Great and unusual chili rellenos.

SONOMA COUNTY

BISTRO RALPH'S

Owner/Chef: Ralph Tingle
109 Plaza St., Healdsburg, CA 95448
(707) 433–1380
Very good. Light, creative fare.
Californian cuisine with a touch
of French.

THE GARDEN COURT CAFE

Owners/Chefs: Richard and
Stacy Treglia
13875 Sonoma Hwy., Glen Ellen, CA
95448 (707) 935–1565
Fabulous breakfasts. Adjacent
antique shop.

JIMTOWN STORE

Owners: Carrie Brown and John Werner
6706 Hwy. 128, Healdsburg, CA 95448
(en route to Healdsburg)
(707) 433–1212
Country store with gourmet deli.
Outside seating area.

JOHN ASH & CO.

Owner: John Ash/Chef: Jeffrey Madura
4330 Barnes Rd., Santa Rosa, CA
95403 (707) 527–7687
Elegant country setting. Excellent
food: fresh, light, regional wine country
cuisine using indigenous produce, lots
of game. Menu changes monthly.

MADRONA MANOR COUNTRY INN

Hosts: Todd and Carole Muir
1001 Westside Rd., Healdsburg, CA
95448 (800) 258–4003
Lovely Victorian home. Food
is absolutely first rate! Eclectic
Californian cuisine. Marvelous wine list.

OAKVILLE GROCERY

Owners: Steve Carlin and Joseph Phelps
Chef: Jeff Mall
124 Matheson St., Healdsburg, CA
95448 (707) 433–3200
Gourmet groceries with excellent
picnic supplies.

RAVENOUS

Owners/Chefs: John and Joy Pozzollo
117 North St., Healdsburg, CA 95448
(707) 431–1770
Tiny (seven tables). Intimate.
Delicious food with an emphasis on
fresh herbs and produce. California
bistro-style cuisine.

SINGLETREE INN

Owner: Bill Chastain
165 Healdsburg Ave., Healdsburg, CA
95448 (707) 433–8263
Popular breakfast place.

WILLOWSIDE CAFE

Chef: Richard Allen
3535 Guerneville Rd., Santa Rosa, CA
95401 (707) 523–4814
Rustic, charming, delicious.
Contemporary American cuisine.
Try the pork chops.

NOTES

PAGES:

13: Stevenson, Robert Louis. *The Silverado Squatters.* (St. Helena, California/Ashland, Oregon: The Silverado Museum/Lewis Osborne, 1974).

15, 50, 64: Chappellet, Molly. *A Vineyard Garden: Ideas from the Earth for Growing, Cooking, and Entertaining.* (New York: Viking Studio Books, 1991).

22: Thoreau, Henry David, "Walking," from a passage "On Cultivation," *Walden Pond.* (1854).

25: Johnson, Hugh. *Vintage.* (New York: Simon & Schuster, 1989).

26: Harvey, Andrew. "Destroy Yourself," *Light Upon Light: Inspirations from Rumi.* (Berkeley, California: North Atlantic Books, 1996).

30: Verschoor, Gerd. *Beyond Flowers.* (New York: Stewart, Tabori and Chang, 1992).

38: Tchelistcheff, André (internationally know winemaker and consultant to the wine industry). Consultation with Donn Chappellet, 1966.

42: Emerson, Ralph Waldo. *May Day and Other Pieces.* (1867).

47, back cover: *The Bible.* King James Version. Song of Solomon 7:12, Isaiah 65:21.

71: Rilke, Rainer Maria. "Sonnets to Orpheus," *The Selected Poetry of Rainer Maria Rilke.* Stephen Mitchell, trans. and ed. (New York: Vintage Books, 1984).

SUGGESTED READING

Berger, Dan and Richard Hinkle. *An Inside Look at Napa Valley: Beyond the Grapes.* Wilmington, Delaware: Atomium Books, 1991.

Johnson, Hugh. *All About Wine with Hugh Johnson.* London: Reed Books, 1995. www.reedbooks.co.uk/docs/mitchell/wine/index.htm

Johnson, Hugh. *Hugh Johnson's Modern Encyclopedia of Wine.* New York: Simon & Schuster, 1991.

Laube, James. *Wine Spectator's California Wine.* Philadelphia: Running Press, 1995.

O'Rear, Charles. *Napa Valley.* St. Helena, California: Papillon Press, 1995.

Robinson, Jancis. *Jancis Robinson's Guide to Wine Grapes.* Oxford, England: Oxford University Press, 1996.

Amador Foothill Winery, Sierra Foothills

MENDOCINO AND LAKE COUNTIES

• Redding

Fort Bragg •
Mendocino •

• Navarro

Red Bluff •

• Ukiah

• Hopland

NOMA

• Geyserville
• Healdsburg

• Yuba City

Calistoga •

Santa Rosa •

NAPA

Sonoma •

• Napa

Auburn •

• Sacramento

SAN FRANCISCO BAY AREA

San Francisco •

• Oakland

• Placerville

SIERRA FOOTHILLS

• South Lake Tahoe

Livermore •

• Stockton

• Sutter Creek

Cupertino •

• San Jose

• Angels Camp

• Modesto